T0196506

Reflections of the Son

Inspirational Poetry

NICOLE L. ELLIS

iUniverse, Inc.
New York   Bloomington

Reflections of the Son
Inspirational Poetry

Copyright © 2010 Nicole L. Ellis

iUniverse books may be ordered through booksellers or by contacting:

iUniverse
1663 Liberty Drive
Bloomington, IN 47403
www.iuniverse.com
1-800-Authors (1-800-288-4677)

ISBN: 978-1-4502-5386-4 (pbk)
ISBN: 978-1-4502-5389-5 (ebk)

Printed in the United States of America

iUniverse rev. date: 8/31/2010

Contents

IN MEMORY

I dedicate this book to the beautiful people who have sewn so much into my life; those who are now absent from the body but present with the Lord; and those who always believed in me and encouraged me to do great things. This book is in memory of you.

Percell Anderson
Lillie Mae Anderson
Gladys Hazel Carter
Doris Griffin
Iris Belinda Hoston

ACKNOWLEDGEMENTS

First, I have to give thanks to my Lord and Savior Jesus Christ who is the head of my life and the savior of my soul. Without Him I am nothing, but with Him I can do all things. I thank Him for allowing me the use of His gift of writing to encourage and inspire others. I am grateful for the great things He has done in me...

To my husband, my best friend, my love, my life, and my supporter, Jermaine Maurice Ellis- thank you for always encouraging me. Thank you for believing in me. Continue supporting me and the vision...

To my daughter, Tiyana, thank you for being my inspiration. I look forward to seeing God use you for His kingdom...

To my son, Jayden, thank you for the cute smiles. I hope you enjoy mommy's book when you learn to read...

To my sister and brother, Chantel Carter and Dennis Carter, III, thank you for always having my back. I love and cherish our relationships...

To my parents, Dennis Carter, Jr. and Trevor Carter, thank you for depositing so much into my life. It is because of those deposits I am able to withdraw some good advice today...

To my best friend, Joi Lewis, thank you for always believing in me and encouraging me. I love you and I bless God for having you in my life. Best friends forever!

To all of my family and friends who have sewn a seed into my life, I thank you for your prayers and support. Thank you for following the TFTD's and the blog daily.

To my sister girls, thank you for fasting and praying with and for me. God allowed us to meet for an appointed time and an anointed assignment. Thank you...

To all of my church families thank you for imparting wisdom into my life and providing spiritual guidance along the way. To my

Gethsemane Baptist church family, thank you for allowing me the opportunity to spread my wings in ministry and fly.

To my Aunt Audrey Byrd, thank you for editing my work with love in your heart and care in your eyes. I am grateful.

To Alfreada Brown-Kelly, thank you for the endless resources and wisdom that you poured into me. I appreciate your selflessness in helping me with publishing this book.

To everyone who decided to buy my book, thank you and I pray that you will enjoy it.

God bless, Nicole L. Ellis

BASK IN THE SON

When was the last time you Basked in the Son
Took time to give your life to the Holy One?
When was the last time you sat at His feet
Listening to His every word so that you could feel complete?

When was the last time you Basked in the Son
And realized that life for you had only just begun?
When was the last time you lifted His name up high
And at the thought of Him began to cry?

When was the last time you Basked in the Son
And took time to realized what He really had done?
When was the last time you fought off sin
In order to allow Christ's sacrifice to continue to win?

When was the last time you Basked in the Son
And realized the battle has already been won?
When was the last time you needed a friend
And found out that He is a friend 'til the end?

When was the last time you Basked in the Son?
When was the last time?
When?

CHRISTIAN FREESTYLE

Lord, through it all you remain by my side;

You give me the will to live instead of to die-

Die eternally-a fate that does not belong to me;

You sent your only Son; now my soul is set free.

I chose to accept you and that is great;

Living my life with you has always been my fate.

Lord, through it all you always remain true;

For that I will spend my life living for you!

THE TRUE IMAGE

I'm weak
when I'm away from you
I'm weak-
A pair means two
I'm weak
For alone I can't stand on my own
I'm weak-
I thought you were there
I'm weak and I'm scared.
Countless nights I cry;
I feel lost inside;
I need you if you're there
I need you to appear
Otherwise I'm weak
    You're strong
    For I never left you
    You're strong
    Because me plus you equals two
    You're strong
    Because I carry you
    There is no need for you to stand;
    You have to go to the place I reside;
    That little place where I sent my Son to die.
    Then open it up and you will see
    You cannot be weak
    If you believe in Me.
    I gave you strength
    When I died for your sins.
    I gave you breath
    That you may live again.
    Step out of your self-doubt
    And lie in your existence
    Your strong because
    That's the way I made you to be
    You happen to be created in the image of
    Me…

A SINNER'S PLEA

Lord, I must say I'm amazed by you
I wake up daily giving praise to you
But I have some questions for you...
How could you do what you did
How could you give your Son for me-
One with flaws from now until you call me
Lord, I'm not worth the air you give.
I sin on site.
As a "sinner" is how I live.
How could you even make me a second thought
Most of my life I was angry
And many times I fought
I'm not worth the food you provide
Some days I wonder why I am even alive
I often hide when it's time to share your word
People don't want to hear from a sinner like me
Lord, why did you die way back on Calvary
Why did you sacrifice a life for me...
Little ole me
Time after time I never realized why I'm still alive
Why your grace has been so sufficient
Why your mercy is beyond me
Lord, I come to you broken
Asking you to forgive me
Lord, save my soul
And set me free
Lord, thank you for keeping me
See, others lost faith in me
Now I realize your love Kept me
Now, I see-without you I would have died
Lord, I love you
And praise you
And will no longer cry
You gave me another chance
To live "Your" life.
Thank you.

SPIRITUAL CPR

Can't breathe?
Try Spiritual CPR:
Consistent in praying,
Persistent in pursuing the knowledge of God,
And
Resistant to temptation.

ACCEPTANCE

It took me a while to figure out, that life is not easy
Living a Christian life is harder than living in the world
I only thought about myself-
Not how I would affect men, women, boys, or girls
My life is a direct reflection of the Son
People hold me to a higher standard
I grow weary
I grow tired
I'd rather run away from my responsibilities
Instead of walking through the fire-
The fire of being different
And standing up for what I believe
I searched for approval of many,
Only to be deceived
I searched high and low for the acceptance of man
And fell every time
Yet You always gave me your hand
Living this life is not easy;
I grow more imperfect each day,
But You promised me that if I love you and believe, you are real;
The enemy will never steal the victory that belongs to me; still
I wanted to be accepted and realized man will never follow through
You're the only one who ACCEPTS me and for that I LOVE YOU!

COME DWELL IN THE SECRET PLACE

You say that you want to Worship Me
And give me total praise
Yet you only go to seek thee
In surroundings emulating a parade
You chase the wind of the world
You search for peace through other's space
You make time for everything else in life
But neglect coming to the secret place
When was the last time you dwelled in my being?
Basked in the righteousness of Me?
Laid aside the schedule of the world
And chose to make fellowship a priority?
You seem to forget in the course of your day
That I am the source, the light, and the way
I invite you into the secret place
So you can become free-
Free from the stronghold of the world
All you have to do is Abide in ME

A PRAYER FOR OUR CHILDREN

Lord, this world is full of heartache and pain
No one is "spiritually" safe without you
People still use your name in vain
Our children are lost and do not know what to do

Parents have given up on guidance
They do not follow your Word,
So the kids lean to the world to form an alliance
They do not want to listen; they want to be heard

Lord, help our children in this world today
Raise up some people who will stand upright
Our children are dying and most often stray
Lord, we give you this battle because we are too weak to fight

Our children are in need of Your salvation
Peer pressure is overwhelming and causes them to fall
We know that you can save a nation
Lord, help the children, help them ALL.

INVITATION TO THE LORD

Lord, I believe I'm ready;
I believe I'm ready to surrender my sins-
Surrender my helplessness
Surrender my hopelessness
Surrender my being
To the Only All knowing
All seeing
All forgiving
All loving
All being God
Lord, I believe I am ready to invite you in-
Invite you into my mind
My heart
My soul
My way of life
My speech
My walk
I do not possess the artistic ability to create
An invitation with cut outs and lace overlay,
Drizzled with glitter and pop outs
But I am desperate to know You
I present myself as filthy rags
Torn
Worn
And given up on by many
This is my invitation to You Lord
Will you accept?
    "I accepted you before you were even born
    My eternal love for you is so great that before your parents knew you
    I sent My Only Son to die-
    To die for the multitude of sins that man would commit
    I've waited on You
    And I knew-
    I knew the day would come when you would invite Me in"

EQUIPPED
Inspired by Ephesians 6:10-20

Living each day from one trail to the next
Some days feel so overwhelming and even complex
Some days seem dark and often times dim
Often as a result of me living my life in sin
I find myself running from the things all around
Searching for a "safe haven" is nowhere to be found
Running from the enemy is not what causes him to flee
On the contrary, running keeps him attacking me
Instead of running I've decided to start to pray
Pray to be equipped, starting with today
I **girded my waist with the truth**
To stand against the lies
I put on the **breastplate of righteousness**
That will help keep me aligned
I placed on my **shoes of preparation of the gospel of peace**
Now I can keep my feet planted and not run to flee
I took up the **shield of faith**
To block the enemy's attack,
Put on the **helmet of salvation;**
I'm almost ready to stand and fight back
Finally, I take my **Sword of the Spirit** which is the word of God
Ready to do battle and stand up against all of the odds
Being sure to pray without ceasing is what you instructed me to do
I am ready to stand boldly and share the mystery of YOU
I used to live my life running away
That has all changed now that I have committed to pray.

BLESSINGS IN A RECESSION

I wake up every morning just to hear the news say
We are struggling from a Recession and they hope it gets better one
  day
Before I accept all the words that I often hear
I pray to my Father whom I trust and love so dear

As I fall on my knees and begin to pray
I hear a sweet voice begin to say
"Be not conformed to this world my child
Participating in something that is not like me is not your style
Death and life lie within your tongue
Do not focus on the world, rather on all of the things that I have
  done
Even with a low income, do I not provide?
Remember it was I who sent my Only Son to die
Although you were once sick, did I not make you well?
Stop focusing on the news and begin to open your mouth and tell-
Tell others of everything that I do and all the joy that I bring
When my Son rose on the third day, He stole death's evil sting
Why do people look at this recession as so bad?
It is during this time that Christians can rejoice and be glad
While the world is panicking and living their lives in fear,
All of my children can praise Me and possess the things that are dear
It is during this time I expose the corrupt and transfer their wealth to
  you
All I ask is that you do not conform but continue to worship me in
  everything that you do
I merely position all of my children to inherit great things
So they can share the love of Christ, shout, dance, and sing
A recession looks bad to the world because they put their trust in man
But you my child, have continued to be blessed because you put your
  trust in My hand
I will continue to shower you with blessings and protect you from the
  evil in the land

When the world sees you prospering be sure to tell them about who I
    am."

As I open my eyes and wipe away my tears,
It is then that I realize I have nothing to fear
God has blessed me in spite of what the world may say,
And I'll be a witness for him forever, starting with today
So when I hear the word *recession* I will begin to smile-
Because I am not of this world, but am my Heavenly Father's child

DELAYED NOT DENIED

The morning starts with your prayer to the Lord
You speak to Him with expectations of greatness-
Greatness for your life and the lives of others
You walk with confidence, tithe and study each day,
Yet you wake up and do not see the pay off of your request that you've
    made
How long do you have to wait?
Did God ignore your request?
These are some of the conclusions that you've come to, at best
Is there something that you did wrong?
Have you been denied the desires and petitions of your heart?
Remember God knew everything about you before you could even
    start-
Start to question or doubt His hand in your life,
Start to put the wheels in motion so that you could make sure you
    live right
God knew all of your requests before they even entered into your
    mind
Consider that your answers are just delayed and not denied
He has to postpone some things in your life
You would not appreciate them now
You would misuse or even abuse them
Damage them or even lose them
He delays your answers and your blessings for His appointed time
He is waiting for you to rely on Him,
So stop thinking that you have been denied
Continue to rise with prayer on your lips
And study His word all the time
Walk with the confidence and great expectations,
And know that your prayers are just delayed and not denied.

FORGIVE THEM

Forgive them Father, for they know not what they do
Words that were spoken so long ago, yet still hold true
Sin resides in our nature
Only by our choice
We can choose to turn away from You or choose to stand and rejoice
Forgive them Father
A plea You made for one and all
Faith and repentance will keep us from the eternal fall
Fall from Grace
And be absent from Your mercy
As long as we put sin first, we will continue to keep on hurting
Hurting from the repercussion of our sin
Caving to our temptations will keep us falling again
Father forgive…
Why do we think it was easy for Him
To forgive those who crucified Him because He disapproved of how
    they lived
Lust of the flesh will lead you to your demise
Lusting over the things that do not keep the **"Christ in you"** alive
Forgive them
Is what He is available to do?
The only thing-He is waiting on is YOU!

GOD STILL PREVAILS

Life will send you stormy days;
Carrying an umbrella does not keep the rain away
Life is full of struggles and pain
Hurtful words often cause a stain
They stain your ego otherwise known as pride
Why do we allow a "word" to keep us from growing inside
There was One who stood the test of time-
One who was persecuted,
Criticized,
And even died.
God knew there would be stormy days,
So He sent His Only Son to pave the way
Jesus is the supreme example to follow
Unfortunately too many of us crawl and wallow-
Wallow in our pity which turns into shame
Too embarrassed to call out His Holy name
Even though we often fail,
God is awesome and He always PREVAILS!

DEATH WHERE IS THY STING?

We were born into sin, surely bound for death
The falling of man came to past by listening to the words
From the serpent's breath
Doubt and intrigue wandered through the minds of God's creation
Eve could not resist and Adam joined in-indulging in the temptation
At first glance the bite sealed our fate-
Banished from glory and destined for hell's gate
Dismissed from God's presence filled with worry within
Life for man would now be flooded with sin
But be not deceived by what man can see
What God can envision is beyond eternity
He sent His Only Son to take the form of a man
Clothed Him in sin so that you and I may live again
Destined to walk the earth and face persecution, betrayal, and
    apparent defeat
Jesus humbled himself even to wash His servant's feet
One with power beyond our comprehension
He withstood the trials and remained in life's submission-
Submission to carrying out what the Father intended all along
Jesus suffered for you even though He knew no wrong
Sentenced to Death for claiming the Father
Even his disciples rejected Him as if they knew him no longer
Beat and abused, mocked and disrespected
The strength of the Lord is more than what spectators expected
A crown of thorns placed on His head
The pain had to be excruciating, I'm sure He wished He was dead
Nails pierced through his hand and feet, blood streaming down his
    side
Imagine the shrieks from the women who cried
"My God, My God why hast thou forsaken me?"
Jesus in His flesh wanted to be set free
He could have come down from the cross and banished us all to
    death

"It is finished" represents the beginning of life spoken from Christ's
  breath
Placed in a tomb to rest in the grave, yet Jesus rose on the third day
"O death, where is thy sting?"
You could not keep Jesus bound for He is the everlasting King
Christ rose with all power in His hand defeating death for you and
  me
He did this all so that we all may have a chance at life more
  abundantly.

PRAISE

Lord, life seems so terribly hard
Each day carries its own heartache and pain
Life is full of ups and downs
Yet I'll still love you the same

Lord, I thank you for the minor victories
These help to keep me strong
They remind me that you are there for me
And with You I can still carry on

Lord, life seems awfully dim
When I fight the world on my own
I know with you I always have a friend
To carry me through the Storm

Lord, no matter what, I will shout out loud
Even though life is a maze,
I will hold my head high and smile
And always give you TOTAL PRAISE!

SPIRITUAL HAIKU

Sin causes dismay
Repentance will set you free
Thank God for the blood

Afraid of failing
It seems like nowhere to run
Stand still; God is here

Still can't forgive them
Hate in your heart will hurt you
Remove bitterness

Step out of darkness
Flee the regrets of the past
Thank God for His light

YOU CALL YOURSELF A CHRISTIAN

You call yourself a Christian
But when you are angry you never pray
You call yourself a Christian
But when God instructs you to speak you refuse to say-
Say the words of encouragement that He has placed on your lips
Because you are too busy carrying your hurt feelings on your hips
Your call yourself a Christian
Because you serve in a ministry
But how can you be effective if you envy the ones who serve Thee
You call yourself a Christian
But all I see is you complain
When you should cry out to the Lord I hear you call people names
You call yourself a Christian
But you are always worried and full of fear
You often listen to the world instead of the Father who speaks in your ear
You call yourself a Christian
Yeah, YOU!
But you've planted seeds of bitterness in everyone you meet
I've been watching you closely to see how I am suppose to treat-
Treat others when they come my way
You've shown me how to turn my back on others and wait for another
    day
Yet, you call yourself a Christian
How could you do this to me?
You've robbed me of the chance to spread love to all that I see
You have been so consumed with your life and your feelings
You failed the assignment that would bring me my spiritual healing
You call yourself a Christian
Yet you live the way that you do
I just wanted to let you know that God assigned me to you
You call yourself a Christian
But you lead me astray
I thought by looking at you I was following the likeness of Christ
I guess I was wrong to say
That you are a Christian

I FELL

I fell yesterday
I fell to the pressures of this world
I fell to sin
And when I looked around, there was a crowd
Kicking me to the ground
I fell
Much like last month and the year before
And when I began to crawl for help
People stood before me and slammed the door
I fell
And, yes, I know that I am down
Yet you call yourself a Christian
But you are so eager to keep me bound
I fell
But did you forget that you fall too
I thank God everyday that the One I serve
Is nothing like me or you
I fell
And Jesus was there to catch me
Dust me off and help me on my way
Repentance gives me another chance-
A chance to make today right
Instead of being so judgmental
Help pick me up and lead me to the light
I fell
But the difference between me and the world
Is that I chose to get up
I will never allow a fallen state to keep me separated
From praying for you
One day you will fall,
But with God's love I will be there not judging you.

TAKING IT BACK

I woke up this morning declaring the victory

I stood firm and confident and told the enemy to flee

I challenged myself to be a better me

To rebuke my sinful nature and fall down to my knees

Kneeling down to pray for my "break-through" today

I claim I have control over what I choose to say

I am taking my moment back

Because it is not anyone's to take

I refuse to let anyone be the cause of why I break-

Break down in dismay or wallow in shame

I claim victory right now in the Mighty One's name

I am taking back my second, my minute, and my hour

I am taking my life back; I truly have the power!

THAT QUIET PLACE

I went to my quiet place today
As I sat in my silence, I begin to hear a sound
The beating of my heart loud like a drum
I could feel God there
I knew he woke me up this morning
I knew he gave me a new day
Sometimes I forget to go to my quiet place
And marvel at God's work
I get so caught up in my temporary insanity
I let the world run me ragged
I let people get me down
I allow the enemy to steal my joy
I allow Satan to keep me bound
Then I sit in my quiet place
I begin to hear that sweet sound
I hear my heart beat
I begin to marvel at God's work-
Me
I begin to allow myself to believe
I remove the world from my shoulder
I remove the enemy from my feet
I sit in my quiet place
Suddenly my heart skips a beat
I sit in my quiet place
I even sit there now
I marvel at the beauty
That took me to be quiet
In order for it to be found…

RELEASE ME

Lord, I've been traveling through this life
Carrying all of these heavy loads
Every trial that comes my way
Makes it difficult for me to continue down this road
The road that will lead me blindly to Your grace
Sometimes I feel like the world is spinning
At an alarmingly fast pace
Release Me
From the bondage that I've allowed to paralyze me
Negative words spoken by others have began molding me
Release Me
From the traps that I make for myself
How I conform to the image of man
Forgetting I have a right to stand-
Stand on the principals of Your Word
Neglecting that I have a voice that needs to be heard
Release Me
Strip me of my pride
Remove the bitterness that clogs my arteries
And the anger that causes me to hide
Release Me
Purge me of the selfishness that keeps me from the ones I love-
Place the type of love and compassion within me that only comes
     from above
Release Me
I'm tired of allowing the enemy to win
You died for my salvation
Now I need to refuse to continue to live in sin
Release Me
A phrase that must come from my heart
Spoken only with sincerity so that my life can have a new start
I'm ready to commit my spirit into your hands
Sometimes you have to allow me to fall in order for me to understand
That You were waiting for me to ask You to
RELEASE ME
Release me!

I'LL TRUST YOU

Lord, my life is filled with hurt and pain
The enemy is constantly attacking me
I sometimes feel like I am going insane
But Lord I'll trust you

I have been hurt by family and friends
Lies and Deceit constantly surround my world
I often wonder when this will all end
But Lord I'll trust you

I have a hard time forgiving the offender
I carry heavy burdens of hate in my heart
I always wonder when they will surrender
But Lord I'll trust you

I pray to you daily and wonder if you hear
Everyone else around me seems to be getting blessed
Sometimes I live my life in fear
But Lord I'll trust you

I trust you because you sent your Son for me
You have loosed my shackles
And because of your love I have been set free
Lord, I do trust you

Although I do not understand all of your ways
I know you can speak to my problems
For it was you who spoke to the winds and the waves
Lord, I do trust you

Lord, I love you
Lord, I need you
Lord, I do trust you
I trust you

PRAY

When you are happy-Pray
When you are sad-Pray
When you are healthy-Pray
When you are sick-Pray
When you are strong-Pray
When you are weak-Pray
When you are brave-Pray
When you are scared-Pray
When you are confident-Pray
When you are insecure-Pray
When you are loved-Pray
When you are hated-Pray
When you are smiled at-Pray
When you are talked about-Pray
When you are bragged about-Pray
When you are lied on-Pray

In everything that you go through-PRAY!

LESSON FROM A CHILD

Lord, I woke up this morning and did not know what to say
I noticed a child today bowing its head to pray
How is it that a child so small
Can cast its cares to you for one and all
How is it that a child can trust so much
When as adults all we do is fuss
Lord, I do not know if you really exist
But watching that child causes me to say, "WHAT IF"
What if You are really true
How can I begin life with You?
Lord, I woke up this morning not knowing what to do
But you sent a little one to show me to pray too
Lord, I come to you as a sinner
I need you in my life to become a winner
A winner for Christ is where I want to be
All because I saw a child praying to thee.

PERCEPTION OF A SINNER

Lord, I hear that you are He
The One who can grant me salvation and set me free
I hear that you are real
A true deliverer who continues to heal
But, Lord, I don't want to be a Christian

All I see is people who proclaim to be of you
Yet as soon as they leave church they disgrace all that you do
Lord, I don't want to be a Christian

Your children are cursing and blaming one another
I even witnessed "Christians" spreading rumors about each other
They sit on my job with scriptures on their desk
But when things are going wrong, they display that their life is a mess
Since you are He who restores and redeems,
Why do your children live as if they do not believe

Lord, I don't want to be a Christian
On the highway they flick me off with a "I love Jesus" bumper sticker
    on the rear
They then proceed to glare at me hoping to instill fear
They sing songs of Praise in the grocery store and every place they are
But complain about everything that sits beneath the stars

Lord, I don't want to be a Christian
Pastors are stealing, church people are hypocrites
I believe I'm better off living like a misfit

Lord, I don't want to be a Christian,
But if I were to change,
Can you lead me to some examples of people who believe in your
    name
Can you show me believers who do not constantly blame

And do not show me "holy" disgraces that are only in the faith for the
   fame
I know no one is perfect
If you are real, then you created me
I just want to see an example of who we ought to be.

INVITATION FROM GOD

God invited me to lunch today
Much like He normally does
I'm just so preoccupied with life
I didn't recognize who it was-
Who it was that quietly called my name
Encouraging me to commune with Him
Knowing that I would never be the same
God invited me to lunch today
And I gladly accepted the invitation.

LIFE HAS NO MEANING

I arose this morning and I felt out of place
I wondered, what would life be like if no one had Your saving grace?
Would people even care about what they would do next?
Living life without you would seem so complex
Fighting and bickering would become the way of life
Living in darkness is all we would know because without you there is
    no light
What would people have to live for without an example like you?
If we had to rely on ourselves, we would not know what to do
We would wander around aimlessly searching for the truth
If we relied on the world, we would have no proof-
Proof of what life is really meant to be
Life has no meaning if you did not set us free
Lord, thank you for the chance to get it right
I come to you stepping out of darkness and into your marvelous light
This life without you was a nightmare for me
My heart grows heavy because this life for others is a terrible reality
Lord, life has no meaning if you were never here
Give me the words to share so that everyone would fear-
Fear life without you in their heart
Lord, compel the unsaved to change and begin a new start
Move the backslidden to get it right
Push the saved to stand up and fight-
Fight for life and all that we believe
Life only exists with You indeed!

LAYING DOWN MY GLOVES

Ever since I could remember I had a fight in my soul
People would try to challenge me, but I would never allow them to
    take hold-
Take hold of the essence that resides within me
I would fight the world with one hand tied behind my back in order
    to defend who I am supposed to be
But somewhere along the way I began fighting YOU
I became resistant to the things that YOU told me to do
YOU told me to accept you; I did
What more do you want from me
Sometimes as a believer I become blinded by the plan you have for me
YOU told me to pray without ceasing, but who can pray all day
I forget that praying keeps me connected to you and helps me to
    follow Your way
I grew so accustomed to fighting those who tried to attack me
That I slowly began fighting even those set out to help me
Lord, I am tired of fighting when I am not supposed to
I am ashamed that I began fighting YOU
I will make this vow to live like YOU above
Lord, today I am laying down my gloves.

MAKE TIME

When I close my eyes to rest
My mind begins thinking of the demands of tomorrow
I begin racing the clock
Wake up
Get dressed
Eat
Get kids ready
Daycare, highway, work
Work, highway, home, church
Highway, home, rest
Where in the course of the day did I make time for You?
You, Oh Lord, who have provided so much for me
You, Oh Lord, who have blessed me with sanity
Clothed me and placed me in my right mind
Where in the course of the day did I make time for my family-
The group of people who depend on me
The ones whose support and love are free
Where in the course of the day did I make time for myself?
Nurturing and rejuvenating the mind and body of me-
Taking time to enjoy the life that you've given me and all of my
    wealth-
Wealth of Your love, compassion, grace, mercy and more
Wealth of my family's hugs, laughter, prayer, and kisses that await me
    at the door
Wealth of the person that lives inside of me
Lord, I promise to make time for Thee, for him, for she, and for me

LOVE, LAUGH, and LIVE

Life consists of series of emotions-
Tears of joy
Tears of pain
To a fault
We allow the negative emotions to move in and take claim-
Take claim over our lives and rule our day
They burrow down on our hopes and crush our nights
We give up on happiness and refuse to put up a fight
We allow bitterness to choke the very life out of our heart
Relationships are ruined before they can even start
Spend more time giving away hope
Love with every fiber of your being
And when things get tough, tie a knot on the end of your rope
Laugh at everything that you see or even say
Do something special with your children today
Spend more energy living this life
Stop allowing problems to cause you to live in strife
Life is short and you have so much to give
Love a lot, laugh more, and more importantly LIVE!

HE SAID WAIT

Far too often I want to do things my own way
I search high and low
I fight with my standards
And my ability to love
I have this thing figured out
Or so I thought
Then I hear a voice say

Just Wait
Wait for a new day
Stop trying to be the creator
Of something you know nothing about
Stop trying to play my part
I am God and will always be
I created you
And I know your destiny
Just wait
Its really not hard to do
As soon as you wait
I will bring HIM to you
Close your eyes and open your heart
Count your blessings
For when they start
You will not have enough room
To hold them on your own
So when I bring him to you
Be sure to make him your Own
JUST WAIT
Because in order for you to see him
You must be patiently waiting
Anticipating
The man I HAVE designed for you-
I need you to recognize
What I have in store for you

So wait
Its already done
I am the Father
The Holy Spirit
And the Son
So now I ask you to listen to me
Just wait
You and your prince will live
Happily…

LORD GUIDE ME
Inspired by James 1:19-20

Ever since I began walking with You
Life has become a struggle
People hold me to a standard
That I was not aware belonged to me
I have to guard what I listen to
Watch how I speak
I even have to be mindful of the places
I go and the people I may meet
Lord, guide me
Life is not easy without you
People test my Christianity
And some days I fear I will fall
At times I get angry with people
For no reason at all
Lord, guide me
Frustration becomes real
Which leads me to speak swiftly
And not listen at all
This formula leads to wrath
And I know that anger causes men to fall
Lord, guide me
I want to live and be like you
Any anger I experience does not come from you
Lord, guard my ears when I am weak
Cause my lips to slowly speak
And delay my wrath indefinitely
So I can produce the righteousness of thee
Lord, guide me

YOU HAVE TO FIGHT

You have to Fight for what is right
Not for what feels good
You have to stand up for Christ
No matter what your current mood
You have to Fight for what is real
Not for what the world creates as ideal
Stand up for more than what you know
Stand up for God because he never leaves you alone
Fight for the King
Do not be fooled by the enemy's schemes
Fight for your salvation
Fight for your freedom
Fight to have a seat in God's Holy kingdom
Fight
You have to Fight
Stand up and FIGHT for what is RIGHT
Make JESUS CHRIST YOUR LIFE and FIGHT!

YOU SEND ME

Lord, each new day you give me another chance
You command my limbs to rise and take a new stance
I often take for granted the things most people lack
The ability to walk, the ability to talk, the ability to react
Lord, you send me a Word
You send me a word showing that I am more than meets the eye
I am articulate, strong, compassionate, and free
Eternally driven to fall into the possibilities-
The endless possibilities that you have afforded to me
Lord, you send me a Word
You send me a word reminding me that my past does not determined
My tomorrow
That you have paid the ultimate price and I no longer have to borrow-
Borrow false hope from the people around me
Rather lean on your Word that reflects the promises of thee
Lord, you send me a Word
You send me a word to share with the World
You instructed us all to tell every man, woman, boy, and girl
That you are Lord
Lord, you send me a Word
And I make this vow not to focus on the how
But to focus on the Now
Now is the time to give glory to your name
Sharing with the lost who have everything to gain
Now is the time to stop feeling sorry for myself
And testify to the world of how we are all blessed
Lord, you send me a Word...

WITH YOUR LOVE

With Your love
I have another chance at life
My past has been erased
I no longer have to live in strife
With Your love
My spirit has been renewed
I no longer have to walk around in bondage
All because of You
With Your love
The enemy will have to flee
You have given me strength to fight
This world can no longer control me
With Your love
I can shine a light
I can swallow up darkness
Because You plus me is ever so bright
With Your love
I have endless possibilities
To love others
As You have loved me
With Your love
I can do all things
With Your love

TRY JESUS

When life is full of fear and doubt
Try Jesus, just give Him a shout
When you need a friend and no one is there
Call on Jesus, He is everywhere
When life is just too much to bear
Lean on Jesus, He always cares.

There is no problem that cannot be solved by JESUS!
There is no challenge that is too hard for JESUS!
There is no friend like my JESUS!
So what are you waiting on to try JESUS?

TEACH ME

Lord, I come to you humbly on my knees
Searching my heart praying for you to hear me
I am tired of living life as a fantasy
Where I am always right and convincing myself
That no one understands me
Lord, teach me-
Teach me how to love unconditionally
Remove the selfish impurities that reside within my me
I come to you exposed baring my heart and my soul
I am incapable of loving if the truth be told
Lord, teach me
Teach me to be a servant like you
Guide me on how to stop depending on myself
And start relying on the things that you do
Love does not exist if you are not involved
Hatred cannot be destroyed if I do not seek to be resolved
Determined to love the way you love me
Lord, help remove the shackles that I allow to restrict how I see-
See the people in my life
Lord, I come to you because I am ready to make things right
Lord, Teach Me
Teach me how to love unconditionally
So that I can represent your love for all eternity.

WHAT WAS HE THINKING?

What was He thinking
When He did that for you
Better yet for me
How could one sacrifice
So much for people who didn't believe
For those who didn't want to receive
It just doesn't seem logical
For someone to love me
Beyond me loving myself
Could you even imagine sacrificing your only child?
Would nature even allow…
Our minds can't even conceive an act such as this
An act of pure Selflessness
What was He thinking
Or was He thinking at all
For to think allows room for doubt
Thinking often causes us to fall
I'm glad I wasn't a thought at all
Rather a feeling that reached into His heart
Which caused HIM to shed his blood
That we may all have a new start
What was He thinking
I don't need to know
I see how much He loved me so.

QUESTIONS

Lord, I come to you wanting to know?
Why on earth do you love me so?
How could you send Your only Son to die
For people who didn't care when He was crucified?
Why did you give your life for those who did not know you?
I do not know anyone who would do that for you.
Lord, how is it that you love a sinner like me?
These are just a few questions that concern me.

Lord ,why is it that you chose this path?
People still sit around and think about you and laugh.
Why do most people sit and mock what you did?
Why do people try to convince me that you do not exist?
Lord, I do not understand why you chose to die for me.
Why my mind is boggled that you set my soul free?
Why did you set me free from the fate that really belongs to me?
Eternity with the devil is where I ought to be.
Yet for me-you had different plan
Why did you send your Son in the form of a man?

Lord, why is it that you sent your Son for me?
How could you watch Him die on Calvary?
Why do you have a better plan for me?
Why did you wipe my slate clean?
Lord, how is it that you love a sinner like me?
These are just a few questions that concern me.

Lord, why did you take those lashings and beatings?
Why did you not cast me out with the demons?
Why do you continue to give me more than one chance?
How can you stand to look at me longer than a glance?
Lord, how is it that you love a sinner like me?
Why oh why, please tell me
Lord, I will never understand you, see,
But these are a few questions that concern me.

I'VE GOT A PRAISE

Woke up this morning clothed and in my right mind
I have movement of my limbs and the ability to see daylight and tell
    time
I've got a praise on my lips
And I refuse to keep quiet
I have so much to be grateful for; why should I sit and remain silent
I have a roof over my head that was designed just for me
A job, healthy kids, and a wonderful spouse, look at the endless
    possibilities-
Possibilities that show His endless love for Me
He paid the Ultimate price way back on Calvary
I've got a praise that I cannot keep to myself
I will praise God for all that He has left
He left His grace that extends way down to me
He left His mercy for a wretch like thee
He left peace that surpasses all understanding
He left hope for a better tomorrow
He left a desire that resides within my heart
He left a chance for me to have a new start
I've got a praise that I wanted to share with all of you
If God has been this good to me, then I know that you have a praise
    too!

MY JOY

This joy that I have

My Lord paid a high price

For me to allow the world to take it

And not even put up a fight

This joy that I have

It's worth more than silver or gold

For me to allow the world to rob me

Of the fortune my joy truly holds

This joy that I have

Was destined specifically for me

For me to allow this world

For ME to allow this world…

How dare I allow this world to take what does not belong to it or me

God blessed me with this joy

And I will cherish it from now and all eternity!

MY LOAD

Lord, my load is too heavy-

Too heavy for me to bear

This world is starting to get me down

No one seems to care

My life is full of trouble

Beyond what meets the eye

I feel like giving up

Then I remember that you are the MOST HIGH

I am coming to you casting my care

Praying for you to give me relief

I want to give up the weight of the world

Before I reach defeat

My child this is all I have to say

I hope that you take note

Your trials are not for you to bear

So never give up hope

When the load gets too tough

Pass it on to me

Remember I am the one who supplies you strength

I will always be there for thee.

NO LONGER THE SAME

God gave me an epiphany
This life that I have been living has never been for me
Salvation was offered so my soul could be set free
And I am assured that I will be with Christ for all eternity
I can no longer live life in sin with no blame
Now that I am saved I am no longer the same

I owe it all to Christ to share His unchanging Word
It is unacceptable for me to hoard all of the blessings that I've heard
God has afforded me the same opportunity as you
But I cannot control others, only what I choose to do
I can no longer keep my mouth closed as if I do not know YOUR
    name
Now that I am saved, I am no longer the same

I look in the mirror and I don't look the same
The way I speak even has changed
I walk taller than I used to before
Things that used to bother me don't discourage me anymore
I don't hang at the places that I used to go
There are even people from my past that I no longer know
With Gods anointing I have forever been changed
Now that I am saved and I believe in Him I am no longer the same.

TEMPTATION WON'T WIN

From the day that I was born it was sin that my life entered in
From the outside it would appear that I was born into a battle that I
could never win
As the years went by, I became intrigued by the things that I could
not have
Everything evil looked good, and I began to long for them really
badly
I lusted for earthly things that would not enhance my life
Rather lead me to an eternal death and days filled with strife
The enemy is tricky and knows of the dark things that fill my heart
But now that I know you dear Lord I do not want sin to cause us to
part
I used to run head first into sin
Treading on the enemy's battle ground with no defense made it
impossible for me to win
Now that I am equipped with your Holy Word
I watch and pray and reflect on the things that I've heard
How I will be blessed if I endure for a night
Standing up to temptation feels better and my heart knows it is right
There is no reward on earth that can fill this void within
I'd rather wait on my eternal crown and continue to resist until the
end
From the day that I was born it was sin that my life entered in
With you on my side, I know that temptation will not WIN!

EMBRACE THE HATERS

They smile in your face and talk behind your back
They misuse you and abuse you and compromise your trust
I used to call them traitors
Now I call them haters
Haters surround me left and right
What they all have in common is they live to start a fight
Some are closer than others
A sister or a brother a father or a mother
They look like strangers and even look like friends
Your most extreme hater can be your next of kin
Haters show up at your jobs, in your churches, and in schools
Some of the well known haters could possibly be you
I used to spend night and day
Praying for God to take the haters away
But without my haters I would not be where I need to be
Haters seek to destroy, but God intended for them to elevate me
My false perception of my haters was a plot by the enemy
To keep me distracted and not operating towards my destiny
I gave them too much power and allowed them to ruin my day
I allowed them to get me flustered and keep me from speaking the
    Words God called me to say
Haters-
They can't hold me down
They hate on me so much that I levitate off the ground
Haters-
They put so much pressure on me
Instead of running, I fall on my knees and grow closer to Thee
I no longer seek to understand why they bring so much havoc to my
    life
Wondering how someone could be so evil and cause so much pain
    and strife
It's easy to love those who are nice to me,
But, Lord, You have called me to love all of my enemies
So to my haters I will no longer hate you

I will no longer lower my standards and trade evil for evil with you
When you curse me, I will speak blessings over your home
When you persecute me, I will pray that God never leaves you alone
You can continue to hate me and I will learn to love you
Everything spiteful that you do, I will not return to you
For God causes the sun to rise on both of us
He even rains on the just and the unjust
Haters continue to hate on me
It was all a part of Gods plan to empower me
I no longer have to understand why it is that you do what you do
Haters, I no longer run
I now EMBRACE YOU!

SANDPAPER LADY

Sandpaper lady, why do you rub me the wrong way
I spoke to you today and you had nothing to say
I made sure this morning I even spoke with grace
Yet you rolled your eyes and had an evil look upon your face
Sandpaper lady, why do you have to be so mean
Of all the colors on the rainbow, you had to choose green
Green with envy over the things God called me to do
Instead of being jealous, embrace how God wants to use you
Sandpaper lady, why do you do what you do
Walking around as if the world and I owe you
Allowing pain and misery to be your fuel,
You turn every suggestion for change into a drawn out duel
Sandpaper lady, who broke you down
Whom did you allow to drag your self-worth to the ground?
Sandpaper lady, let me encourage you
Never allow the hurt from your past to cripple you
It's time to strip yourself of all your pride
And embrace the love of Christ that lives deep inside
Tap into the beautiful strong woman that you are destined to be
Release your anger and that mountain of anxiety
"Sandpaper lady" is not a title filled with fame
I haven't had the opportunity to meet the "true" you
Hello, what is your name?

YOU ARE

Somewhere along the line
Life abused you
Hurtful words were etched in your mind
And a false sense of reality confused you
All the words that are spoken
That are filled with negativity-
Happen to be a misguided view of your reality
You are strong
For the strength of the Lord is with you
You are beautiful
For you were traced in the image of God
You are articulate
For the words you speak come from above
You are caring
You are nurturing
The gentleness of your hands cover your children, your husband, and
    your friends
You are wise
Because you are filled with the instruction of the Lord
You are determined
Failure is not an option in a child of God
You are a queen
You sit above the rest
Yet you humbly acquiesce to the request of the Lord
To submit
To refrain
To speak life, hope, and love
You are woman
Destined to be free
Allow the light of Christ
To continue to shine in you
For all the world to see
You are somebody special in the Lord.

WHAT I SEE

Lord, when I looked in the mirror, all I could see
Was a stranger staring back at me
The nose looked familiar and even the hair,
But deep within my eyes I didn't recognize who was there
The world began criticizing me
People tried to steal my joy and dignity
All of this was done in an effort to bring me down
Subconsciously I started to believe that I was like everyone that was
    around
I began to search Your Word to reveal who I was destined to be
Genesis 1:27 reminded me that I was created in the image of THEE
With this revelation I was no longer bound
By the self proclaimed haters designed to tear me down
I have assurance of who I am suppose to be
Now when I look in the mirror, I recognize who is staring back at me
I hold my head high and remain humble within
I am constantly reminded that sin does not have to win
My outward appearance may look the same,
But now when I look in the mirror I see a change
Thank you for always staring back at me
I love you, Lord, for creating me.

IT'S NOT ENOUGH
Inspired by Nehemiah 1:11

It's not enough to simply ask someone to pray-
Pray for me
Pray for my needs
Pray for my desires
Yet I refuse to fall on my knees and pray for others
It's not enough to simply ask the Lord to listen to my words-
Words that fall from my lips with an eagerness to be heard
But I overlook the petitions from others
I constantly make everything about me
As if God cannot help another
It's not enough to simply ask for someone to pray for me
Hoping that if I have enough prayers lifted up on my behalf
That the Lord will fulfill my needs
Prayer is a privilege that was given when Christ died for me
But Christ died for all to be connected to the Father
So who am I to operate selfishly?
Lord, your Word has revealed to me to pray for the lost, the sick, and
    everybody
Listen to those who desire to fear you so that they can be set free
Hear the petitions of others as I intercede to Thee
Let each and every person prosper who is in my heart and on my
    mind
I vow to make praying for others a valuable part of my time
It's not enough to simply ask for someone to pray for me
I find so much joy when I pray for others and live unselfishly

THE SIMPLE THINGS

I woke up this morning and inhaled
Air filled my lungs
Blood flowed through my veins
Heart rate was normal
My limbs slowly began to move
As my brain dictated the day
Washed my face,
Brushed my teeth,
Clothed my body,
Lotioned my skin
Placed shoes on my feet with no assistance
Walked down the stairs
Fed myself and saw the family on their way
Fell to my knees and began to pray
"Lord forgive me for I have sinned
I often get to the end of the day
Limiting my thanks to you to a few
But the reality is I could not pray if it was not for the
Simple things that you do
Forgive me Lord; I make this vow
To tell the world of you,
And challenge everyone to reflect on the Simple things
That you do."

TURN DOWN THE VOLUME: SILENCE THE NOISE

You told me that I would never make it
She told me that I will one day be hated
He told me that marriage is just a piece of paper
They told me that I would be destroyed by haters
You tell me to give up now because the task is too great
She tells me reaching my goals are not in my fate
He tells me to give up; I'll never win
They tell me that I will never conquer sin
Then I reach my hand to the circular instrument that controls sound
I begin to turn the volume down on you, on her, on him and on them
I must silence the noise that tries to rob me of my destiny
I must silence the noise of the insanity
I must silence the noise so that I can hear when my Father speaks to
    me
Do not feel ignored
It's just time that
I
Silence
The
Noise…

VENGEANCE IS MINE

I will never understand
How someone can disappoint a child
And call himself a man
You know my heart lies deep with my girl
God blessed me with her and made her my world
I try to fight the demons within
Refraining from becoming the sinner again
It becomes tough not to explode
It's hard to know the feeling unless you have walked down this road
You make empty promises and never pull through
You leave my child staring at the phone
Waiting for your call to come through
You make a vow to be a better man
Then all you do is bring more children into this land
You disappoint her time after time
You say you will see her this weekend
But we both know that is a lie
You say you live for her
But you live for yourself more
Its is taken God to hold me
To pray for my girl to endure-
Endure your broken promises
Over and over again
Then I stop listening to myself
And listen to God within
I pray for strength and for this drama to end
God made a promise and cannot lie
I heard God say, "Vengeance is Mine"
So now all I can do is pray for mercy
Because when God sends His wrath
He will make all my enemies bow down
And I do not want to be in his path
It took some time to realize why
But God has said, "Vengeance is Mine".

WILL YOU WORSHIP ME? A QUESTION FROM GOD

I blew breath into your body
I spoke life and you now exist
I carry you through the bad days
And hold your hand through the good
But I still have to ask, "Will you worship ME?"
I sent my Only Son to die
For sins that were not His own but yours
I watched Him endure persecution,
Lashings, and beatings-
A penalty that should be yours,
And yet, I still have to ask, "Will you worship ME?"
I brought you out of the land of Egypt
Your Egypt was depression, drunkenness, promiscuity,
Infidelity, malice, pride, murder, lies, drugs, bitterness,
Envy, jealousy, robbery, and more
I became your salvation
However, I am the One you constantly ignore
Will you worship ME?
I took you out of bondage
I offer a means to save your soul
Sweet communion is what you can have with Me
From now and past the days when you will grow old
I extend peace, love, and joy to your life
I cover you with a hedge of protection
I lay grace and mercy at your feet
Yet, I still have to ask, "WILL YOU WORSHIP ME?"
I released the chains and set the captives free
But some of you insist on allowing sin to control thee
I will love you for all eternity;
Please don't wait too late to worship ME.

YOU ARE APPRECIATED

Often times I allow my busy day to consume me
The hustle and bustle of work, family, and friends preoccupy me
Forgive me for allowing things and people to steal my attention away
    from Thee
It may seem like all that You do for me and provide for my family
    goes unnoticed,
But on the contrary, I feel You when the world lets me down
I hear You when sickness fills the air and knocks me on the ground
I see You when no one else is around
When the wind blows past my face giving me a rejuvenating burst of
    air,
I know that's You
When the rain falls on my face and I can tell that it's cold, I thank
    You for allowing me to feel
When tears fall down my face and somehow they vanish before they
    hit the floor
I know that it's Your hand that carried them away
Often I get lost in time and space
But never do I forget about You
Your love for me brings a smile upon my face
Just merely thinking about your saving grace
I get so overwhelmed when I think about all that You do
Dear Lord, I appreciate YOU!